New B

Andreas Koutsoudis

Presentation by *BookLeaf Publishing*

Web: www.bookleafpub.com

E-mail: info@bookleafpub.com

ISBN: 9789358314199

First edition 2024

The Expressionist

When fear finally dissipates from the furnace
inside,
The strangulation of expression ends and my
muteness is gone,
My voice comes back to me
and calmness of mind returns,
Then self esteem and fluidity of thought create
improvisation.

When I gather both paint and brush, and think of
an idea, or maybe not,
Music is played signalling a return to peace.
I begin with the first brush stroke and
satisfaction,
In the flow of spirit and energy I'm guided by
outer power,
I look back and I'm amazed at what I did.

When I paint, I paint with fire,
I paint with gusto and passion,
Energy and pace,
What you see, is what's inside me,
I let it flow without judgement,
I let it flow.
I practice over and over,

Proliferation brings with it wisdom,
I practice over and over,
The exhilaration never ends.

When I cry out,
When I hope for inspiration,
I know the listener is present,
I know there'll be a kind response and an act in perfect discernment,
Fore my passion is a good one and the picture is true,
Whether I use Prussian blue with lemon yellow and white, or scarlet with effervescent gold,
I know if I'm happy and energised, I've done a good job.

When I sit back and absorb the moment,
I realise again and again that life is very simple,
We complicate things,
But, when we follow our heart and feel the moment we live life,
Our picture, our voice, it speaks a thousand words,
The furnace still burns bright,
But the fear has gone!

Irrepressible

I'm a hurricane, I'm a lightning bolt,
I'm a exploding volcano, I'm a revolution
personified, you cannot contain me, you cannot
box me in, you cannot label my life, I will never
be what you want me to be or think I should be,
I'll be what I want to be!

I will not be restrained,
I will not be controlled,
I will not change my words, my actions or my
thoughts for any man or anything!

Im a new horizon, I'm a blast of sunshine, a
rising star, there's method in my madness, I can
only but go far.

There's no cliché in me, I'm not a has been or
was, I'm not over the hill or washed up.
I'm fresh, I'm new, I'm ongoing development and
ongoing progression,
I bear my cross with a smile on my face, with
determination and a song of grace,
I'm poor as poor, but my inner being is richer
than rich,
There's no glitch in me,

There's nothing wrong in me,
If you see it,
That's your problem,
That's your fault,
That's what's wrong with YOU.

I'm my own law, my own rule, and that's cool,
It's cool to be different,
To be unusual,
To be strange,
You may point the finger or gesticulate your hand my way,
But, it's my way or no way! Understand?!

Everybody has flaws and weaknesses,
But some people dig deep and grind in life like a lion, and their heart roars with might,
As to live in life is to fight and fight, and FIGHT!

I'm a giant, a monolith, but you'd never know,
As my countenance is humble and my head is low,
The greatest is the least, but the fire burns ferocious within the soul,
To get to where I need to get,
And your evil ways and the evil one himself will never stop me,

I will never break my stride to get where I'm going,
Your daggers will not kill me because I'm God made,
God tells me what to do and how to live my life,
God gave me the power,
Gave me the power to be good,
Gave me the power to be strong,
Like an athlete I'll keep running and I'll keep rowing to get where I'm going,
And nothing and nobody will stop me!

The Good Cause

Sharp as a blade,
My words can break bones,
Soft as a kitten,
But, twice shy once bitten,
The irrevocability of your actions,
Leads to God and man entwined,
And you will feel the bitter pain of the spiritually blind.

Strength from within and sight from above,
The language of genius philosophy and the spoken words of love,
A cup of coffee or three and adrenaline driving through rippling muscles,
The actions of Zeus, a lightening bolt to your psyche,
The mythical element is hear to confuse, but the reality of life is to grind and bruise,
To fight and hussle, when all give up,
When they know the truth, they keep their mouth shut,
Or they pump up the evil and pretend it's you,
But, morality and God work for the good few,
And no matter what they say,
You are defended by what's right,

As evil never wins any, ANY fight!

Evil is weak in every form,
Cruelty, deception and charm, only do harm,
It's like pride in Chess,
If you care about winning too much,
You will lose every time,
Inside the game matters,
Whereas if the game doesn't matter, but you play with love,
You play with freedom and might from above,
Win, lose or draw it doesn't matter,
But, life is not a game to play with the mind of others, destroying their will power and their sanity, like a check mated King,
I have feelings, I'm not a toy or a thing.

The genius of life is goodness,
This is the key,
If you see this in front of you your entire life you will see a man born not in great power, but in humility.
The contradiction in life is greatness is small and meek, and has fragility, but is here to shuffle the pack,
It is peaceful but with powerful words put in action,
Walk the walk, not with a poker face, or a hidden hand,

But, always have your hand revealed,
As the truth is the strongest form of defence,
It goes straight to your heart,
Here you'll find what you truly need,
Without lies, without hiding, without a mask, the task in life is to be who you are meant to be,
Be yourself and be good,
Pull up your pants and take off your hiding hood,
Be strong, don't be wrong,
Fight and wage war for the good cause,
And never EVER pause!

The Storm and the Madman

Without high winds, but with supreme light,
Adam and Eve, the first faithful beings were
fashioned from the earth by God's own hand.
The Genesis of life and life of the creator tells us
that humility only comes through suffering,
And only through suffering can truth be learnt
and shown,
Fore the creative man, the artist, the most
beautiful art is to love, and to give your gifts
truly and humbly.

The creative man like a mathematical genius
first swirls gently,
Like a nonchalant finger calculating the
impossible,
It deciphers dust and siphers through branches
like blood through brachioles, fore blood
circulates the body through the heart,
This flow of invisibility is like a stream of
algebraic equation, a trigonometry of
pythagorean proportions,
A slight movement of brow, a change of
expression displays an air force blow to the
enemy,

The enemy with the nerve to suggest he is weak minded,
The nerve to say he's unintelligent,
Fore he is undoubtedly touched by that tincture,
His hand dealt delicately placed derangement,
The freak, the crazy, the schizophrenic man, who overcame the complexities of life like a hurricane shattering the very core essence of negativity and stupidity,
Rigidity and frigidity,
To become a tornado of liquidity and fluidity,
With supreme invincibility of faith.
Overcoming the storm is strength,
analysing simply and with the freedom to look beyond the usual and the same to see the unique and the originality of the art of life.

By breaking his mind, the storm challenged his pysche,
In the aftermath the destruction and debris left behind became a learning curve unparalleled,
to create is to challenge the status quo,
to create is expression of life,
to create is breaking down impenetrative barriers that a wind cannot break.
The mind is the powerfullest force,
To seek that which hasn't been sought,
to find that which hasn't been found,
To show the truth in art like no other,

For a man destruction occurs for creation to
happen,
a creation only a madman can create,
his reward is his own being living a good life.
He was shaped for art,
like a whistling wind chisels rock
and nothing and nobody can halt this.
He has the lever and can move mountains, and
he found the lever himself through the grace of
God.

The Good Artist

We are like a stone being chipped away at,
tap after tap,
until beauty is revealed.
Life shows us this,
It shows us true talent and true strength,
We are chiselled,
We are broken down,
We are hammered,
For our own good.

Our eyes are opened and we gather grit, steal and iron,
Our hearts are warmed,
Our minds made gentle,
Our creativity enlightened,
Our fires made burning,
Tap after tap,
Pieces are broken off,
Our weaknesses are chiselled away.

We crack and crumble,
We are pounded down,
Each breakage reveals
strength after strength,

An inner core of resilience and determination
that only the tenacity to never give in will bring.

The artists stone made good and humble,
closer and closer to that final image,
that final destination.
He revels and delights at the anticipated
achievement in his own gift,
It is brilliant music to him,
The tools of art are the heart and soul, and all
that is inside is displayed for all to see,
What matters is the shear exhilaration,
The joy and reward,
People may marvel, people may stare,
Genius or madness who knows,
Tap after tap into his life and mind, and spirit.

We are only damaged if some beauty is not
revealed,
We are only damaged if the artist is unhappy,
We are only damaged if we damage others,
The Good Artist only nurtures his power, his
spirit is high and his power is happiness, his
power is to reveal the truth that lies inside him,
after all weakness is of material, strength is
unseen.

Soul Searching

They fall at the wayside,
The gutter is nowhere to live,
They take and take,
When to survive you give.

They bend and they break,
The break is life long,
They stop and think too much,
Recovery has gone.

They lose their faith,
Money is all they need,
Their opinion is king,
Their wealth and their greed.

Pride is the Devil's possession,
Deception is vanity,
The humble are gracious,
The weak fight for sanity.

When the time comes to meet glory or doom,
Is your conscience clear,
Did you do your very best,
Or did the demons your heart sear.

Did the devil win you over,
Or were you held close by life,
Were the Angels with you,
Or did death rule with scythe.

Look deep into your mind,
Discover your true self,
Is your soul protected,
Is truth your only wealth.

In the end you will know the meaning of why we are here,
Your souls destruction or everlasting history,
Love is our purpose and the way to live,
Live for the victory of life's divine mystery!

The Life Beyond

Beware of men who fear the light, as beyond the darkness of rolling hills and twisted trees, distorted pebbles, jagged rocks and sharp mountain edges and all the demons of the earth, the fresh air smells sweet and the water pure, the earth good and nourishing, and the light is as bright as can be.

Beyond that which we can see and comprehend with sight,
where hope lives the light shines brightest,
Here faith is strongest and the truth dwells upon high.

In this land of faith, of the unseen, dreams are awake and living, the past is alive, the dangling of the rope of death is severed, life beyond life ringing an endless delightful chime of hope and faith is seen for the first time before your very own eyes. No longer will you cry tears of torment, but overwhelmed with tears of the beauty and joy you see.

The hopeless and powerless now are hopeful and powerful,

The downtrodden and belittled now are risen and mighty,
The miserable and low now are elevated and exhilarated.
The clouds are no longer dark,
The air is light, the flowers and the leaves are bountiful and colourful beyond imagination.

Light is here,
fore darkness blinds, but now we can see,
We can see the good and the great,
We can live the fulfilled life,
The cherished life,
All those tarnished days and the murkiness in our minds is now clarity, like the purest stream of the freshest water.
Like the song of the Nightingale, we hear and its beauty never fades.

The child afraid of the dark
was never afraid of the light,
Beyond the horizon innocence and truth are intertwined,
The child's instinct is the blessed reality now realised,
As fear no longer exists,
As perfect love hast cast it out,
And only love can make the life beyond this darkness shine!

Inner Strength

His eyes caught me, weak, pale and distant. Yet within the wrenching of his solar plexus was pressure, but also depth.

Fore the depth of his will power remains, from outer chaos to internal peace, as spirit is far greater than wasted skin, and the eternal always outlasts the frail body.

His eyes are flowers, Chrysanthemums, late in opening and always startling in presence.
It never ends his presence, the three colours of the petals, dazzling white, yellow and orange, flames and fires of the imagination and creation itself.

He awakens, rising to the sky and beyond, like the sun, but greater, like the moon though always full, like a tidal wave without harm and like emotion without sadness.

His eyes begin the rainbow and the end too begins with freshness and vibrance of colour. The freshness, the taste, so sumptuous in the mouth. Honey and dew of nectar, though flavoursome is far beyond the senses, in the very depths of the soul.

Inner strength makes all have life.

During Lockdown

Once upon a time in the middle of the lockdown, I had a dream, I saw the meaning of life 2 metres infront of me. The picture didn't lean in or linger, or stop and stare, it was just there.

I understood it immediately, its shadow, its form, it was neither crestfallen nor forlorn, nor torn. It was applied in victory, not blame or scorn, it was the peak of existence, the essence of man, in times of trouble it does what it can, that which you cannot do.

The mighty feel it, so do the weak. The rich, the poor, the low and the peak.
It is freedom,
It is life,
It is that you can see.
It is Inside you,
It is rest,
It is the love inside me.

All around is weakness,
All around are the dead,
All around are the scattered and worn, the torn.
All around is disease and isolation, the devastation of desolation.

But this, this, is far greater than that.

It is the strength beyond strength,
the life beyond life,
It is the untouchable human spirit,
the God given power of will.

Fore inside we burn,
A ruptuous inferno,
Molten steel.
A Granite strong carving,
A living stone,
A straight chiselled path to the great unknown,
A woven tapestry of magma,
A range of insurmountable mountain,
The beautiful life of the life giving fountain.

It is the gushing forth of glowing white light
which gives
the overwhelming gift of sight, to the blind and
to the sighted.
fight the good fight,
Wage the right war,
Inside your heart and inside your mind,

As, It is love.

That is which gives hope.

Control of the masses

My heart,
soft and warm,
will always be my own,

My smile, will always effect another with
sincere and loving kindness,

My thoughts, like birdsong will always salute
the truth with vibrants and clarity,

My humility will never be touched, nor cracked
by enemies.

You can't break my faith,
You can't destroy my beliefs,
You can't kill me,
My soul is intact,
My spirit rises like a roaring lion,
My mind is free.

Our freewill remains for eternity!

Never will power overwhelm the people!

It is not a matter of anarchy, rebellion or
uprising,
Its a matter of giving glory,
not to a man in power,
but to that which gives us the greatest freedom,
that of inner strength!

Confinement

You're a prisoner at home,
A prisoner at war,
The invisible enemy,
Is outside the door.

Tension and stress every single day,
Frustration and agitation is still on the way.
Loneliness kills you like a blade,
Isolation like quick sand, makes you fade.

You can't breath,
You're drowning,
Your mind is enclosed,
You're frowning,
Your bubble is made of stone, but you're not alone!

Every boat is the same,
But, your not a number,
Your not a clone,
Your free to express!
Even in this crazy, screwed up mess.

Its not easy to stay calm,
Not easy to remain sane,

Our freedom has gone,
But, it will return again!

Don't bury yourself in a grave,
Don't give up and die,
but rather
Dig a deep trench,
Strong, wide and long,
A trench for the weary,
A trench for the strong!

This trench,
Is a bed of creativity
A nest of activity
A hive of productivity
A opportunity to display ability and to show
your tenacity.

You're a soldier of adrenaline,
A warlord of energy,
Electrifying power surges
From your body,
To annihilate the enemy,
With the power of tenacity!

The tenacious Improvise,
The tenacious adapt,
The tenacious are flexible,
The tenacious overcome,

The tenacious don't give up,
but have already won!

God's Grace

God's Grace is rare, they say,
But happens every second,
The meeting of artistic minds,
The striking of creative weapons,
He makes us cry, but with meaningful intent,
He makes us laugh and is always meant,
The making is in fact our own, but he knows it will happen, he knows why, how, when and where, he knows when we walk and when we stare.

When we fall, he picks us up,
When we hurt, he heals our wounds,
When we are crushed and can take no more, he lifts our heart off the floor and holds us gently in his embrace, wiping our brow and a kiss on our face.

We let life get to us all too much,
We think about nonsense and such and such,
But, when we focus on his way,
We see the light of another day,
We see that his ease lightens our weight,
And gets us out of our mental state,

Our stress and strain, and pain will leave with prayer and hope, and when we just believe and cope.

Indeed faith is enough to save our soul.

Show Yourself

I believe in breaking the status quo,
I believe in rising above the machine,
I believe in dismissing the powers that be,
I'm no yes man,
I do not agree for an easy life,
I do not accept for harmony's sake.

I go down, but I'm never out for the count,
I awake, I rise and I fight back,
My instincts are to survive, to live and to flourish,
By nourishing my mind and body, I never let myself succumb to the outside,
I feel it, but it passes.

To strive and struggle is life,
Walls get in the way of clear sight,
But we fight and fight for what is right,
We hussle and tussle and battle our way,
Breaking down walls,
Destroying darkness,
Eliminating evil,
Eradicating disturbance and confusion from our minds by being a helping hand.

Back on my feet, will intact,
passionate and fighting,
Speaking out and not hiding,
Never internalising, but
Showing my guts and then glory follows,
I don't vibrate, I shine the light of faith!
I don't have a frequency, I'm on a higher plane to paradise!

I hold onto hope,
I will take away your hurt with love,
I will always help,
I have freedom and I will show it in my mind and actions,
Nothing holds me back,
My strength is pain,
The pain that creates humility,
The humility that comes from faith,
The faith in the Truth.

The Small Victory

For those who fail to empathise,
Lightning shatters your dreams,
For those who are empty and tired from wasted effort,
Will remain so until a change of heart,
For those who do not want to understand another,
A bomb detonates through your impervious facade,
Fore humanity is for love not hate,
It is to guide not to fight,
To embrace and not break.

But, those who get broken love more,
Crushed by another, they strive for the greatest wish,
The wish for humility and justice to win,
Their strength is sight,
To see the right from the wrong.
Delicate in mind,
But strong in will, their heart cannot be still until the Sun's rays shine on the good cause.

The best fight may appear as a loss,
It takes time to emerge,

But this victory is higher,
It is engrained,
It is who we are,
It is this which truly dominates the world,
The will of truth.
All appears as bleak and damaged, and corrupt,
But the will of truth always has victory.

Life is not a game to meddle with emotions,
It's not a front to conquer souls
And have them as a trophy,
Life is precious love and kindness,
It is this kindness which enables the humble man to win,
As the small victory is the conquest over the dark hearted,
This is strength a man has,
And lasts from the break of the dawn of time to the neverending souls in peace.

The Cross Road

It's the cross road of life,
Decide or regret,
Do I chose cold or do I chose heat,
I'll listen to my heart and decide with my feet.

This way or that,
Left or right,
Is it flight or is it fight,
I'll fight for my heart, I'll fight for my love, I'll fight for my faith, I'll fight from the start.

It's the new chapter in life,
The middle salute,
Will I die or surrender to life,
Will I give in or forgive,
Will I accept or be brave and live.

To live isn't to squander your chances,
It isn't to test your luck,
It isn't to risk your life on triviality,
To live is to be bold in your belief, strong in your strengths, faithful in your fight and tenacious with your time,
It's a chance to build and a chance to align.

I'm on the bridge,
Half way across,
Much water has passed beneath and I remember the gains and the loss,
I got to keep busy living,
I got to start with the first move,
I can't think about death,
I got to keep positive
And think of my first breathe.

Life is too harsh to be barraceded in,
I got to explode forth,
I got to jab and jab my way back in,
I got to take chances and counter punch sin,
Fore this is the way of mercy,
I got to pray and not let evil win.

The cross road is here,
Self reflection or share my heart,
Superficial or a meaningful bond,
Am I trash washed up or is new life at the other end of the shore,
I must dig deeper than ever before,
I must realise my blessings and hold onto that which I adore.

Memories

Memories fade,
No longer sharp, no longer certain,
Focus goes and one is foggy at best,
When the blade is blunt,
Then begins the true test.

The mind is gone,
But the soul is revealed and the heart remains,
Without judgement, without stains,
An empty shell it seems, a disturbed demeanor,
But the childlike person couldn't be cleaner,
Cleansed and pure,
And for this their path is made sure.

Straight to the abode where no challenge is,
Where no demand is,
Where no threat or conflict is,
But only peace and only assurity,
An everlasting moment of clarity,
And ever so beautiful and fruitful,
And only growth and life exist,
And death has gone for good,
And only abundance and only gratitude,
And there you sing and dance, and rejoice,
Hand in hand,

Brothers and sisters forever,
At last, at last that darkness has gone!
And the Sun will shine on you!!

The Skilled Sailor

Many men sail in smooth seas,
Many men swim and sink,
Many men achieve nothing through ease and
gain little from a calm tide.

The skillful man sails in the roughest waters,
He sails through waves of trauma bubbling upto
the surface,
He sails through and passed breakdown and
depression,
He sails through failure, up and down to calmer
seas and to eventual Victory of Light in his eyes
and mind!

The resilience of the Sailor means he sees the
bigger picture,
The entire beauty of the oil on canvas,
He cultivates like a gardener and celebrates
growth and learns with appreciation,
He accepts the critics and puts the power of
effort before his talent,
10,000 hours practice to be proficient?
He puts in double, triple, more and more!
Training the muscles of his body and brain,
cultivating his grit, determination and steel,

His mentality is growth,
His mindset is strong,
His attitude is clear,
He redefines Genius fore his experience is a
Hurricane that came and went!

He survived,
He learnt so much,
He can only succeed,
When he's low, when he panics, when he's
confused, when he's stifled,
He gets through those deep waters time and after
time,
Because he knows he can!

He's not alone,
He knows his weaknesses are shared,
He's blood and bone, he's not made of stone,
When he hears "I Am With You"
He rejoices,
The seas calm,
The sun rises,
It was worth the struggle, worth the pain,
Worth the effort,
There is everything to gain...

The Hand of Love Saves you from drowning
every single time!

The Cradle of love

Haunting, but beautiful, frightening, yet special,
The kaleidoscope of uncommon genius to crack any code stems from love of the heart,
Incredibly smart though with a softness and a kindness untold,
Until the terrifying psychotic episode did unfold,
Then the rare story unravelled for people to behold.

This schizophrenic is a beautiful man, with a beautiful mind,
A soldier of mentality,
A psychological warrior overcoming cerebral torture to see what others do not,
Not the delusions, not the hallucinations and voices in his mind, but the artistic, creative, unfathomable ability to decipher numerical oddities rendering the odd and stigmatized to normalized and harmonized, and kind.

The movements and circling of pigeons is a game, that brings fame and Nobel Prize, no surprise that love and genius with that Aristotelian tincture of madness and sadness, brings unparalleled brain power,

No sour taste,
No regret,
As love conquers iniquity and frailty to display the facts set,
Strengths through electrocution to find the solution,
Strengths through overcoming medications and drug filled injections,
Strengths through morality, mortality and insanity.
Poetic justice and injustice unhidden withstanding cruelty, true and empathetically purposed,
Without riptide and corseness, but built with gentleness and warmth, and genuine, not pride and a thick hide, but humanly kind.

As the diploma was given, the painting sold, the applause and the handshakes over,
He thanked the bond of love that got him past being stripped of life,
The embracing cradle of love gave him a power greater than any other,
to give love back.

The Living Rose

I'm a thirsty fiery Rose,
Who needs to be watered to survive,
The beauty is there,
I just need love and I just need care,
Delving deep into my soul,
Delving deep into a black hole,
That's where I used to be,
But I was never blind, I could always see,
My soul was always old and bright,
The hole is always filled with warmth and Light.

I thank the trauma of my childhood,
I thank the bullies and cheaters, and liers,
I thank the psychopaths and Narcissists, the backstabbers, the fakes and frauds,
The ignorant and arrogant,
The loose ties and cut cords, The ego centric ex cons, who see themselves as the light of the world, but who can't stand themselves or admit who they really are, I've seen it all, I've come very far.

I'm grateful for the hateful, but also for the blessings of friends and loved ones,
For the genuine and respected,

The honest and the modest,
For those who stumble, but are humble,
The fiery Rose is one of those,
As he was chosen and he chose,
He chose to forgive and rise, and he arose, he arose!

Trust is key, but so is truth and reality,
if you think you are pure, you're wrong,
If you think you're a genius, you're deluded,
If you think you're the devil incarnate, you're far from the Truth,
If you believe you're a Saint, that's for others to judge, so don't go there,
Life is unfortunate and unfair,
But is also kind and mild,
Life like time can stop and stare,
It can be wicked and it can be wild.

The contradiction that is truth,
That the boastful are the weak and the humble are the untouchable,
That gratitude is never truly felt until regret brings more Roses to the grave,
Tears speak the truth as true
sorrow is heartfelt,
Prepare for true life,
The life beyond,
The life that sings joy and fulfillment,

The life of the living Rose,
Fore He arose, He arose, He arose!

The Human Heart

Mechanical excavation of deep earth reveals golden treasures, all matter of priceless antiquity's and relics, but none more marvelous than the revelation of the human heart.

Ask a simple question and arousal of depth and determination is explained...

Hello dear sir, how are you?

Well...

Let me begin...

I'm by the dark waters, next to "Capability Brown", heading in the same direction as his bronze statue, to the bridge over troubled water. An uphill road, but beautiful and serene, the waters are calm, the Geese likewise, people come and go, running and walking.

Like refuse collected on the edge of the river, I at times feel discarded, but even out of waste, flowers grow and flourish.

It's a cool vibrant day and life is good, growth is difficult, but it always occurs, whether you like it or not. It's when with the force of my will and my fire that the greatness happens, and always without pondering.

Strength and sinew of mind over matter, doing without effort when you become proficient through effort, is practice makes perfect.

Whence I was glum, now filled with fortitude and Iron.
Whence I was dwelling, now I am living.
Whence I pondered, now creating.
Whence there was a boy with dreams of greatness, now a man with knowledge of what greatness is, a kind and loving heart, fore this is life, secondary are achievements and accolades.

Strive to the heart and true growth occurs, when you cry you see things, true things, it's not gold that matters, or power, but a compassionate life.

The Pioneer

Like a firebird,
Like an angel of light,
He encapsulates the human spirit,
Touches the soul,
The very essence of life.

This can never be taken away
from the heart or the memory,
Fore imparted from him to you in his silent steps
is hope,
The chiming bell of hope,
The music of wonder and power,
Not history or philosophy,
But eternity.

With a tincture of the mystical and madness,
with rhyme and reason and an elusive clean
sweep, he cannot be touched or changed,
He is.

Like a wild white horse,
He can't be stopped or restrained, his light
spreads and fills the lives of others without
pause,

With notes of destiny in his song he crushes corruption and injustice and sets sail to higher ground.

The artist is the pioneer,
Playing the fiddle of life,
The brush stroke of humanity and genius,
To touch one soul is a gift and can never be taken away!

Milton Keynes UK
Ingram Content Group UK Ltd.
UKHW050640150424
441175UK00014B/571

9 789358 314199